*Greater T
available in Ebook and Audiobook format.

Greater Than a Tourist Book Series
Reviews from Readers

I think the series is wonderful and beneficial for tourists to get information before visiting the city.

-Seckin Zumbul, Izmir Turkey

I am a world traveler who has read many trip guides but this one really made a difference for me. I would call it a heartfelt creation of a local guide expert instead of just a guide.

-Susy, Isla Holbox, Mexico

New to the area like me, this is a must have!

-Joe, Bloomington, USA

This is a good series that gets down to it when looking for things to do at your destination without having to read a novel for just a few ideas.

-Rachel, Monterey, USA

Good information to have to plan my trip to this destination.

-Pennie Farrell, Mexico

Great ideas for a port day.

-Mary Martin USA

Aptly titled, you won't just be a tourist after reading this book. You'll be greater than a tourist!

-Alan Warner, Grand Rapids, USA

Even though I only have three days to spend in San Miguel in an upcoming visit, I will use the author's suggestions to guide some of my time there. An easy read - with chapters named to guide me in directions I want to go.

-Robert Catapano, USA

Great insights from a local perspective! Useful information and a very good value!

-Sarah, USA

This series provides an in-depth experience through the eyes of a local. Reading these series will help you to travel the city in with confidence and it'll make your journey a unique one.

-Andrew Teoh, Ipoh, Malaysia

\>TOURIST

GREATER THAN A TOURIST- SPRINGFIELD ILLINOIS USA

50 Travel Tips from a Local

by Taino Costales

Greater Than a Tourist- Copyright © 2019 by CZYK Publishing LLC. All Rights Reserved.

All rights reserved. No part of this book may be reproduced in any form or by any electronic or mechanical means including information storage and retrieval systems, without permission in writing from the author. The only exception is by a reviewer, who may quote short excerpts in a review.

The statements in this book are of the authors and may not be the views of CZYK Publishing or Greater Than a Tourist.

Cover designed by: Ivana Stamenkovic
Cover Image:

Image 1: https://commons.wikimedia.org/wiki/File:Downtown_Springfield.JPG
Éovart Caçeir at English Wikipedia [CC BY-SA (https://creativecommons.org/licenses/by-sa/3.0)]
Image 2: https://commons.wikimedia.org/wiki/File:Springfield_Cityscape.jpg
Katherine Johnson from Springfield, IL [CC BY (https://creativecommons.org/licenses/by/2.0)]
Image 3: https://commons.wikimedia.org/wiki/File:Springfield_Illinois.jpg
NASA Astronaut [Public domain]
Image 4: https://commons.wikimedia.org/wiki/File:Gfp-illinois-springfield-capitol-and-sky.jpg Yinan Chen [Public Domain]

CZYK Publishing Since 2011.
Greater Than a Tourist

Lock Haven, PA
All rights reserved.

ISBN: 9798608168376

>TOURIST

>TOURIST
50 TRAVEL TIPS FROM A LOCAL

BOOK DESCRIPTION

With travel tips and culture in our guidebooks written by a local, it is never too late to visit Illinois. Greater Than a Tourist- Springfield Illinois, USA by Author Taino Costales offers the inside scoop on Springfield. Most travel books tell you how to travel like a tourist. Although there is nothing wrong with that, as part of the 'Greater Than a Tourist' series, this book will give you candid travel tips from someone who has lived at your next travel destination. This guide book will not tell you exact addresses or store hours but instead gives you knowledge that you may not find in other smaller print travel books. Experience cultural, culinary delights, and attractions with guidance from a Local. Slow down and get to know the people with this invaluable guide. By the time you finish this book, you will be eager and prepared to discover new activities at your next travel destination.

Inside this travel guide book you will find:

Visitor information from a Local
Tour ideas and inspiration
Save time with valuable guidebook information

Greater Than a Tourist- A Travel Guidebook with 50 Travel Tips from a Local. Slow down, stay in one place, and get to know the people and culture. By the time you finish this book, you will be eager and prepared to travel to your next destination.

OUR STORY

Traveling is a passion of the Greater than a Tourist book series creator. Lisa studied abroad in college, and for their honeymoon Lisa and her husband toured Europe. During her travels to Malta, an older man tried to give her some advice based on his own experience living on the island since he was a young boy. She was not sure if she should talk to the stranger but was interested in his advice. When traveling to some places she was wary to talk to locals because she was afraid that they weren't being genuine. Through her travels, Lisa learned how much locals had to share with tourists. Lisa created the Greater Than a Tourist book series to help connect people with locals. A topic that locals are very passionate about sharing.

>TOURIST

TABLE OF CONTENTS

BOOK DESCRIPTION
OUR STORY
TABLE OF CONTENTS
DEDICATION
ABOUT THE AUTHOR
HOW TO USE THIS BOOK
FROM THE PUBLISHER
WELCOME TO
> TOURIST
1. Exchange Pleasantries
2. A Mighty Network
3. Downtown Activity
4. Downtown Traffic
5. Nostalgia Parks (And Food!)
6. Personal Favorite Eateries of a Home Resident
7. Span of Lodges
8. Finance Management
9. Fun with Friends
10. City of Lincoln
11. No Car? No Problem!
12. Marijuana Laws
13. Ideal Time of Year
14. Groceries and Practical Shopping
15. White Oaks Mall

16. Practical Sanitation
17. First Aid (Just in Case!)
18. Other Emergency Items
19. Quick Dropbox Access to Info
20. Amateur Photographer Hour
21. VPN Up
22. Importance of Power Banks
23. Flexibility
24. Let the Locals be Your Tour Guide
25. Hoogland Center for the Arts
26. Illinois Symphony Orchestra
27. SAA Collective
28. AMC Theaters
29. Nightlife (Further Explained/Boondocks)
30. Adams Wildlife Sanctuary + Henson Robinson Zoo
31. Great Water Parks for the Summer
32. Upscale Furniture Stores – Consign and Design
33. Abraham Lincoln Attractions (More) Abe Lincoln Rail Splitter Statue
34. Modern Art Strewn Throughout – Acts of Intolerance Sculpture
35. Structural Beauty of Bicentennial Plaza
36. Support our Local Sports Teams
37. Old State Capitol
38. Dana-Thomas House

>TOURIST

39. Abraham Lincoln Memorial Garden
40. Central Illinois African American History Museum
41. Lincoln's New Salem
42. Vachel-Lindsay Home
43. Botanical Gardens
44. Elijah Iles House
45. Edwards Place Historic Home
46. Illinois State Museum
47. Governor's Mansion
48. Lincoln's Tomb
49. Mr. Accordion's Grave
50. Come Back Again Soon!

TOP REASONS TO BOOK THIS TRIP

Other Resources:

Packing and Planning Tips

Travel Questions

Travel Bucket List

NOTES

>TOURIST

DEDICATION

This book is dedicated to those seeking to find their place.

ABOUT THE AUTHOR

Taino Costales is a tenured creative writer and artist. He loves to write when he's not making music and loves to make music when he's not writing. He is a true-to-the-core representative of Springfield, born and raised, who aims to one day represent the city in some manner from within the writing field.

Born the son of Falconer Billy Blackwolf Costales and accountant Elizabeth Costales, Taino was raised to become tangibly literate from an early age. One of Taino's greatest motivators in life is his close family and friends, who he helps to positionally elevate alongside his own self.

>TOURIST

HOW TO USE THIS BOOK

The *Greater Than a Tourist* book series was written by someone who has lived in an area for over three months. The goal of this book is to help travelers either dream or experience different locations by providing opinions from a local. The author has made suggestions based on their own experiences. Please check before traveling to the area in case the suggested places are unavailable.

Travel Advisories: As a first step in planning any trip abroad, check the Travel Advisories for your intended destination.
https://travel.state.gov/content/travel/en/traveladvisories/traveladvisories.html

FROM THE PUBLISHER

Traveling can be one of the most important parts of a person's life. The anticipation and memories that you have are some of the best. As a publisher of the Greater Than a Tourist, as well as the popular *50 Things to Know* book series, we strive to help you learn about new places, spark your imagination, and inspire you. Wherever you are and whatever you do I wish you safe, fun, and inspiring travel.

Lisa Rusczyk Ed. D.
CZYK Publishing

>TOURIST

WELCOME TO
> TOURIST

>TOURIST

The Illinois State Capitol as seen from Capitol Avenue

An image of Downtown Springfield with a view of the State capitol

Photography of Springfield taken from the International Space Station (ISS)

Present Capitol building, built c. 1868–1888

>TOURIST

"Illinois surpasses every other spot of equal extent upon the face of the globe in fertility of soil and in the proportionable amount of the same which is sufficiently level for actual cultivation."

– Abraham Lincoln

A learning grounds of endless avenues, Springfield successfully manages to encapsulate the active and bustling life of its contemporaries, such as Chicago, coupled with the sense of community found in smaller towns.

With a lenient standard of living, along with a "bang-for-your-buck" approach to many of the locally owned and loved businesses and suites, Springfield manages to strike the perfect balance.

Our bustling city provides a manageably learning curve for those new to leaving their home city. Likewise, Springfield also holds a range of subtleties within its charm, beauty and strange disposition.

A city for those bold and ambitiousness enough to dare beyond the status quo, Springfield is sure to have something to appease people from all walks of life.

Springfield Climate

	High	Low
January	43	22
February	48	27
March	58	35
April	68	45
May	76	54
June	85	63
July	89	67
August	89	66
September	81	58
October	69	47
November	57	36
December	46	26

GreaterThanaTourist.com

Temperatures are in Fahrenheit degrees.
Source: NOAA

>TOURIST

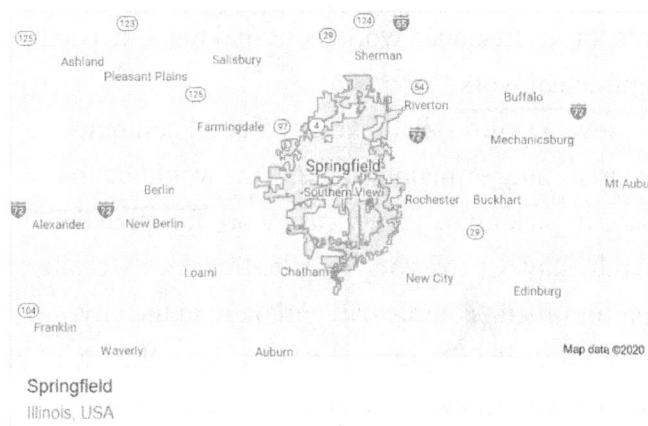

Springfield
Illinois, USA

1. EXCHANGE PLEASANTRIES

In a similar manner to many small towns, don't be surprised if people on the off chance pass a friendly smile and hello in passing (occurs more frequently downtown and in public settings).

Make sure to reciprocate this and join in on the general sense of fraternity provided here.

Springfield proudly lacks both the pressure and the casual disconnected provided in some regions such as Chicago and New York.

You will find this fact typically consistent in most of the community and public service centers, as well as with local businesses. Springfield is quite the hotspot for freelance workers to find much-needed contractual work.

Have a skillset that revolves around computer programming or maintenance? This would be the place to pick up relatively easy work for quite the healthy pay. Check your favorite freelance website or app for on-site contractual work here in the city.

Cold-walk ins aren't a bad idea as well, as here in the city they show a greater drive and initiative.

2. A MIGHTY NETWORK

Not only is Springfield an active permanent residence for many, the hub-like city also serves as a midway point for many important events and people. This includes business meetings, performance arts, and politicians of a high caliber.

You never know who you'll meet or who you'll get to see perform in Springfield, so at the very least keep an eye out on tour dates! Many amazing acts perform in surrounding Chicago and St. Louis territories as well, with both places not being horribly far out of reach from the capital. This is, provided you have efficient commute arranged ahead of time.

>TOURIST

3. DOWNTOWN ACTIVITY

The number one most important rule of Springfield would just so happen to be: downtown is where everything occurs.

Although you may find interesting pockets here or there with worthwhile potential, the quintessential occurs and will be hosted downtown, or at the very least on the Northside.

For those new to Springfield, it would be recommended to avoid housing projects on areas such as the Eastside of town, as these areas have a higher rate of crime in comparison to the rest of Springfield. Places to avoid would include S. MLK Drive and Poplar Place Apartments.

4. DOWNTOWN TRAFFIC

As is per usual with many a city, downtown happens to be known not only for its nightlife, but also for its half-asleep drivers.

The rest of Springfield fares a lot better than downtown in this regard, so just be visually aware. Being the safe driver is what counts.

Feeling drastically uncomfortable about traffic, or just aren't a big fan of driving in general? There are many third-party services that are relatively to be trusted, allowing you to commute for a reasonable price without restriction.

Don't let these words intimidate you regarding Springfield traffic, it is just good to use common sense while driving here, as it is anywhere else.

The backroads of Springfield allow for long, comfortable drives with minimal interference. The city's backroads also give access to a lot of surrounding towns, as well as exits onto and off of the highway.

5. NOSTALGIA PARKS (AND FOOD!)

The parks of Springfield, Illinois hold their own unique simplicity that echoes nostalgia for both home residents and tourists alike. From your first breath of the Fall air, to mountain biking all through various paths, the outdoorsman in you will clamor for more of the city's rural sites.

>TOURIST

Lincoln Park, Washington Park, and Carpenter Park all provide their own established settings, each one structurally and aesthetically different than the last.

I suggest visiting them in the order listed. This will allow an optimal view of the contrasts. Each park is ideal for different activities as well. For example, Lincoln Park and Washington Park are excellent for fishing and frisbee golf, while Carpenter Park is more suitable for hiking and cycling.

All three parks are conveniently located relatively close to many transitional areas in the city, thus leading to an expansive catalog of food establishments to choose from. More parks exist in Springfield besides them but are typically of a much smaller demeanor. Satellite villages will contain at least one of their own namesake parks, as well.

6. PERSONAL FAVORITE EATERIES OF A HOME RESIDENT

To keep things simple, we'll chop it up (narrow it down) to three restaurants that I feel encapsulate the positives of Springfield. These listings are in no order of rank.

Jolly Tamale is quite possibly the most enjoyable quick-service Mexican food in all of Springfield and its surrounding areas. With a tightly knit work crew, established guests and admirable formalities for what it is, I highly recommend Jolly Tamale for a quick bite to eat. My go-to would be the Southwestern Steak Fajita Wrap. I would almost go as far as to say it has severely impacted my life, for the better.

Mario's Pizza is another excellent spot to grab a bite to eat at, serving outstanding homestyle Italian cooking here for over 25 years. Amazing for a party night at the Wyndham when you and your friends need something made with a little bit of love.

Lastly, you must check out Star 66 Café. Open 24/7, their service is beyond concise and qualitative.

>TOURIST

As for their menu, well, let's just say it's about the equivalent of ten of these tip books.

There exist more higher-end eateries within Springfield, those are just my personal quick choices.

7. SPAN OF LODGES

Throughout the city you will find an endless span of lodging options, ranging from low brow to luxury.

Hampton Inn, The Ramada, and The Wyndham are all excellent high-end choices that manage to be simultaneously affordable. Plan on throwing a party you plan on remembering but will manage to forget? These would be the spots for such activities.

I would stay away from any motels of a questionable disposition, but that's just me. They well serve you fine most likely if you find yourself in a bind. Many lodging options are available on the interstate routes to Springfield as well.

Smaller scale lodging options include the Inn at 835 Boutique Hotel, State House Inn, and the Midtown Inn. These three are well-received in terms of accommodation rates, cleanliness and staff service.

8. FINANCE MANAGEMENT

ATMs, coin-to-cash machines, and bitcoin tellers exist all throughout Springfield, especially downtown. If you're in a bind and need to access checking or savings accounts, you should have little trouble doing so. You should be able to find most major banks somewhere in the city.

Many facilities within Springfield use up-to-date technology in term of electronic cash transfer.

To be extra safe, feel free to take an additional backup debit or credit card with you as well for tight situations only.

A good rule of thumb for tourists in Springfield would be to only carry larger amounts of cash with intention. Understand where you're going and what you plan on spending the money on in a timely manner? Carry your cash as you please. However, as with any city, it is not the brightest idea to carry large amounts of money on you, especially downtown during afterhours.

>TOURIST

9. FUN WITH FRIENDS

Springfield is very much so a location built around socially oriented activities. If you plan on traveling here, make sure to bring friends and family along with you! If you choose not to, don't worry, as there are plenty of good-hearted locals to make acquaintance with as well.

Many seasonal events, amusement parks and attractions exist within Springfield, with there being new places of interest every time you revisit! If you're not from the Midwest, do take care to note new events, festivals and otherwise that may be coming to our wonderful city!

10. CITY OF LINCOLN

The name Springfield is often associated with the accomplishments of Abraham Lincoln. A portion of downtown is practically themed around him, with there being a multitude of facilities created in honor of his name or with the purpose of elaborating upon his lifetime accomplishments.

Some of these sites would include the Abraham Lincoln Presidential Library and Museum, the Lincoln Home National Historic Site, as well as the Lincoln Monument Association.

Each of these areas holds incredible historical significance regarding Abraham Lincoln's life, serving as a true sight to behold for history buffs and casual adventurers alike.

11. NO CAR? NO PROBLEM!

"Shoe-friendly" is a good adjective I would use to describe Springfield. If you happen to have no personal means of transportation arranged for yourself, and likewise would also rather not deal with outsourced taxis as well, have no fear. Downtown, although vast in size, is neatly organized in such a manner that many points of interest, hotels, and eateries are all within reasonable walking distance of one another. Theoretically you could arrive here from the airport, call a taxi/Uber to take you downtown, and then basically be set for the rest of your trip.

This fact stays relatively consistent throughout the entirety of Springfield, even its more rural or deserted parts. Chances are that if you find yourself an eatery, there'll be about five more and a Walmart within a mile's distance of where you're at. If you're familiar with city commutes, you will find yourself agreeing with this statement. Although not as foot oriented as places such as Chicago or New York, Springfield still has its place for those who aim to truck on foot.

12. MARIJUANA LAWS

On June 25th, Illinois governor J.B. Pritzker signed into effect a new legislation that would make said state the 11th to fully decriminalize marijuana.

This decriminalization law takes effect on January 1st of 2020. In direct correlation with this, many new medical and recreational businesses are preparing to setup shop both in downtown Springfield and otherwise.

Many predict that there is a possible upcoming "boom" for Illinois in terms of its taxable cannabis industry.

The law applies to smoking within private households only and is prohibited in public places aside from to-be designated spots.

13. IDEAL TIME OF YEAR

The activity-optimal season in which to visit Springfield would be during the latter end of Summer (middle of August). Large events such as the Illinois State Fair and Twilight Parade garner participants from all over the country and then some yearly, truly bringing life to the streets of the North-end.

Atmospherically, nothing can replace the energy that is given off during this community-driven season for Springfield. Everyone seems to be having a lot of fun during "fair season", with the routine's end almost being saddening by the time it's all said and through.

>TOURIST

14. GROCERIES AND PRACTICAL SHOPPING

One of the most convenient things about being in Springfield is the fact that typically, everything you'll ever need will be within eye's distance. Mini-malls and plazas galore, it's trivial to knock out multiple errands in one go during your stay. This fact echoes true throughout the ENTIRETY of Springfield, not just one portion or in one concentrated territory.

Google Maps will be your best friend when it comes to navigating towards the more obscure and nuanced businesses that reside. Most major grocery chains, including Hy-Vee, Walmart and Aldi's all exist throughout the city. These are followed by more regional establishments such as Schnucks Markets Inc.

If foreign markets are your thing, you're sure to satiate all your seafood needs in Springfield. Some of the owners of upper-scale Oriental restaurants in the city also own a handful of accompanying Asian markets. Each of these foreign markets is built on their reputation for fresh, high-quality ingredients of any genre or variety.

JCPenney, Macy's and TJ Maxx all exist in Springfield as well, upholding more than reasonable prices on clothing. Outlets for more popular brands exist in Springfield, as well as on its outskirts plus surrounding cities. These Asian markets import goods from throughout the world as well, not just specifically Asia.

15. WHITE OAKS MALL

A staple of Springfield culture and activity would be the White Oaks Mall, located at 2501 Wabash Ave. Host of 77 unique stores, shopping centers and eateries of high-quality, this entertainment center is sure to have everything for everyone.

Better yet, there also happens to be a large amount of surrounding commercial centers adjacent to the mall as well. If you're having trouble finding what you're looking for at White Oaks, you're sure to find it nearby!

>TOURIST

16. PRACTICAL SANITATION

Plan on spending time all over the city and downtown? Make sure to pack amenities such as hand sanitizer and sunscreen. The temperature in Springfield varies in correlation to time and place, as does the cleanliness. Smart preparation never hurts and only helps.

Additionally, purchase travel-size packets of detergent beforehand in order to make it more convenient and practical to clean your clothing. This small addition to your arsenal could make a great difference in terms of your comfort in the long-term.

When frequenting murkier places you may be unfamiliar with, remember that it takes about fifteen seconds of exposure to hot water in order to kill bacteria. Washing your hands, applying soap and then washing your hands again aids in the application of soap. Some things you get away with in your place of origin you may not get away with in other areas. This could be due to a sense of micro-immunity.

17. FIRST AID (JUST IN CASE!)

As with any other city, I recommend having a first aid kit with you. On the off chance that one of your children get hurt, you'll be able to manage the situation in a timely manner.

When you're traveling solo, you may find this less necessary. However, if you are traveling with a spouse and kids, first aid materials will indeed come in handy.

One should likewise carry medicines and antihistamines such as acetaminophen, Benadryl and Dramamine.

Secondary items could include small flashlight or headlamp, waterproof matches and super glue. Each provide their own various uses in emergency situations.

An important backup note for this tip would be to carry two first aid kits: one that remains in the vehicle and one that remains on your person/in your luggage.

>TOURIST

18. OTHER EMERGENCY ITEMS

Rule of thumb states that in times of emergency, it's always good to have an active secondary cell phone on you or another person within your party.

Currently, it is easy to pick up a prepaid Android smartphone with all the works for as cheap as $20 or $30 dollars. Even for the stingiest of travelers, this minute investment serves in both the short and long term.

Another item (or series of items) that flies under the radar would be multi-purpose shoes. Have shoes for different contexts, as you wouldn't want to wear loafers to a skate den, or skate shoes to a formal. Disposable t-shirts (muscle fit is my personal preference) are also incredibly practical and useful.

Worried about vehicle or housing stability on your own part? Don't forget to pack a few perishable goods and bottled water, as no matter where you travel, you never know when you might need them.

19. QUICK DROPBOX ACCESS TO INFO

One way to store secondary info that you may need quick access to on the go while in the city would be to use Dropbox. You can access and store files universally from any device, phone or computer. Documents are shared and accessed lightning fast, even with a lackluster connection.

Dropbox allows for quick management of documents that contain things that may overwhelm you to have constantly rotating in your head.

Other cloud services work similarly in function, as does an offline word processor for laptop or phone.

Documents containing more critical date can be stored in an encrypted file, such as an Evernote with said encryption settings enabled.

Electronic peripherals such as thumb drives and external hard disks can prove useful for travel as well, especially for artists such as writers or musicians. Nowadays, you can acquire something in the >500gb range for $30-50, occasionally at a substantial price drop depending on where you are shopping.

>TOURIST

20. AMATEUR PHOTOGRAPHER HOUR

Springfield is an excellent place to sharpen your amateur photography skills. The flow of the city lends to natural shots with an architectural balance that varies throughout the city.

From our heart-warming parks to our rustic urban scene, an endless catalog of themes can be portrayed and cultivated.

The city also serves as a hotspot for music video shoots and the like. There is plenty of work to be found with the local artists that reside within Springfield.

Whether on top of a parking garage filming the sites of the city, or just at a local waterbed enjoying the scenery, there are plenty of picture-perfect moments to be found in Springfield.

21. VPN UP

If you happen to be someone who relies heavily on electronic fund transfer through multiple accounts, it would be best to subscribe to some type of paid-VPN service.

When you're using hotel or public Wi-Fi, there is a liability there that your info can be intercepted by somebody else and used for malicious purposes.

Surfshark, ExpressVPN and Vypr are a few layered choices for extra protection over your accounts, no matter what network you're on!

What specifically does a VPN do to enhance the user-end experience? Well, for one they secure local traffic while browsing on public Wi-Fi. This means that you are protected from having your data intercepted by a third party as your device communicates with the network.

VPNs also bypass ISP-related filters and restrictions, which proves especially helpful for tourists! They also provide ample security for those who transfer data via torrents.

>TOURIST

22. IMPORTANCE OF POWER BANKS

With increases in modern technology within the last decade, power banks have become more and more popular. This is within good reason, of course, as the practical service they provide is helpful in all applications.

Power banks of all different budget ranges can be found at local supermarkets and electronic boutiques, such as Walmart and Best Buy.

To use a power bank, you plug into an outlet or adapter just like you would a phone/phone charger. The power bank stores "x" amount of power, and when the power bank is removed from the outlet, it can then be used to power any number of devices.

These devices are made further useful by their sheer size and portability, allowing one to be able to conveniently carry a selection of them in their bag or purse without any noticeable detriment.

Make sure to try and network with some of the photographers around here as well. Springfield is an excellent city to network in and you can truly come across some interesting and skilled characters on your journey.

23. FLEXIBILITY

Springfield, being the eccentric city that it is, does not necessarily run according to your "time" and preference. Thus, your trip here will be made much more enjoyable if you approach it with a stress-free, non-stringent tone.

This applies likewise not only to your own tone, but your accessibility to events around town. If something gets knocked off schedule by outside forces, just remember, there's always something to do in this city!

You should have little trouble finding supplement attractions if things go awry in one way or another. Keep in mind that most people find themselves in bogged-down situations due to their own self-imposed restrictions, so again, stay flexible with both schedule and self.

>TOURIST

24. LET THE LOCALS BE YOUR TOUR GUIDE

Happen to have targeted questions? Feel free to ask any of the locals around to help fill in the blanks. Many people in Springfield are honest and hard-working, willing to help you out of positions of trouble, or at the very least serve as an accurate point of reference.

Becoming comfortable with the locals is another way to help build your social skills, as well as grow your feel for the community in Springfield.

An example would be, let's say you're having trouble locating the delicious Italian restaurant, Saputo's. You come across the Illinois State Museum and decide to take a short rest there. Feel free to ask staff and visitors where Saputo's may be located, as they're likely to give you accurate details on the location's whereabouts. They may even be willing to share their subjective reception with you as well.

25. HOOGLAND CENTER FOR THE ARTS

Originally constructed as a masonic temple in 1909, the facility that is now referred to as the Hoogland Center for the Arts has quite the evocative legacy.

Nowadays, the Hoogland Center exists as an 80,000 square foot community performing arts center that hosts three separate major performance rooms, as well as many other spaces for accommodation.

Hoogland is an epicenter for cultural displays, so make sure to check out what's going on there daily! You never know what's in store.

Conveniently enough, Hoogland is also located next to many other facilities of convenience. These include Obed & Isaac's Microbrewery + Eatery, the Springfield Muni, and President Abraham Lincoln Hotel.

Most art communities within Springfield find themselves time and time again contributing or performing within the Hoogland Center, cementing its status as an ever-changing nexus of artistic life.

>TOURIST

26. ILLINOIS SYMPHONY ORCHESTRA

Gracefully aging to its 27th season, the ISO has received universal acclaim for its many performances as well as accomplishments in orchestral music.

The ISO's performances tend to revolve around Springfield, as well as Bloomington-Normal.

A cascade of scheduled concert arrangements exists for the ISO annually, including four Symphony Orchestra concerts, two Chamber Orchestra concerts, as well as many seasonally themed performances.

Seeing the ISO perform is a reoccurring element of many prolific tourism lists regarding central Illinois. The reputation of ISO supersedes that of many other orchestras.

27. SAA COLLECTIVE

The modern art examples to be found in Springfield are occasionally nonpareil. The SAA, or Springfield Art Association Collective, serves as no different. An easy exhibition schedule is available right off the bat from their official website, making it simple to get an idea of what's going on in these surroundings.

The commercial sales gallery and generally well-received professional hub had humble beginnings as the Prairie Art Alliance in 1979. Originally built upon women's suffrage, the PAA changed to nonprofit in 1985, and became what it is known as today in 1995. This is due to correspondence with the fact that men began contributing to exhibits and the association.

Throughout the years since its establishment as the SAA, it has been known to occasionally make expansions, typically every seven years or so.

28. AMC THEATERS

The dying art of the movie theater doesn't have to go so soon. Make sure to keep up the tradition of viewing some new cinema while you're out and about in Springfield. AMC Classic and regular theaters serve as a perfect intermission between busy errands to trips at the water park

>TOURIST

Multiple AMC locations exist scattered throughout Springfield, making it easier to find one than lose one.

AMC Classic has a wide variety of bonus deals and cashback opportunities regarding their services, so make sure to take advantage while you can. This proves even more so lately, as theater sales have been on a downtrend in the last decade.

Who knows, you may find yourself experiencing the underground resurgence of the Golden Age of Cinema! Or maybe you'll just have a good time with friends and family.

Not a fan of AMC? Don't worry! Many other theaters exist in Springfield's satellite territories.

29. NIGHTLIFE (FURTHER EXPLAINED/BOONDOCKS)

The nightlife in Springfield isn't only restricted to downtown, you know. Still located on the Northside, you can find wonderful music venues and bars such as the Boondocks, waiting happily to satisfy your craving for food, alcohol, music and fun!

Boondocks is Springfield's largest live music venue eatery, holding many State and nationally recognized awards. National and local acts are welcome at the Boondocks. If you're a performing artist of any genre, try and have a chat with the staff there. They would be more than happy to schedule you if you take your work serious and are ready to rock the show, no matter the genre (albeit they are rock oriented).

Located on N Dirksen Parkway, just like with many other places in Springfield, you're likely to stumble across it sooner or later. When you do happen to stumble across this incredible establishment, you won't regret it.

Boondocks Pub also hosts private events, allowing for scheduling either in person, on the phone or through computer form. Boondocks touts itself as the perfect location for receptions, graduation parties and birthdays.

>TOURIST

30. ADAMS WILDLIFE SANCTUARY + HENSON ROBINSON ZOO

Two beautiful spots in Springfield to observe wildlife are the Adams Wildlife Sanctuary and the Henson Robinson Zoo. Each fill in the blanks for one another, as they do have quite the stark contrast.

The Adams Wildlife Sanctuary is managed by the Illinois Audubon Society, a non-profit organization in Springfield that specializes in wildlife preservation. The sanctuary is home to restored prairieland as help promote the thriving of wildlife in the area. This was also done in order to widen diversity.

The Henson Robinson Zoo, open seasonally, is another good spot to go and appreciate wildlife. Although not too far off from what you would see at a fair, accompanied by similarly overpriced goods, the Henson Robinson Zoo is still an excellent facility. The staff there are quite knowledgeable and share a great passion for the animals that are under their care.

Make sure to stop by both spots at least once each before departing the city! Animal enthusiasts and rights activists alike will find themselves smiling in the presence of such passionate staff.

31. GREAT WATER PARKS FOR THE SUMMER

Knight's Action Park is an excellent water park location in Springfield that provides fun for friends and family of all ages. With there being a large variety of rides, slides and other activities, you're sure to satiate your boredom at Knight's! The establishment is an excellent venue for kids' birthday parties.

Amusement parks not your type of thing, but swimming is? Don't worry! Springfield is home to numerous community pools and swimming facilities of an upper standard. These include Veterans Memorial Pool, Eisenhower Pool and the Nelson Center. You will find each of these locations to be quite affordable, especially when taking into consideration the season passes available that are often on reduced offer.

>TOURIST

32. UPSCALE FURNITURE STORES – CONSIGN AND DESIGN

Consign and Design is the most reputable furniture store in all of Springfield. Touted as a safe, friendly and affordable place to acquire furnishings, be sure to make a stop here! Consign and Design could prove especially helpful if you are from a state with a high standard of living. You may just find yourself able to purchase furniture of the same quality in your state, but for half the price!

You may be able to locate Consign and Design's location easily just be seeing the steady stream of customers coming in and out of its 2332 Denver Drive headquarters. There truly isn't a finer furnishing store around in the city.

33. ABRAHAM LINCOLN ATTRACTIONS (MORE) ABE LINCOLN RAIL SPLITTER STATUE

This one is for all my fans of kitsch, and otherwise avant-garde art out there. Located on Sangamon Ave from within the State Fairgrounds lies the menacing effigy of Honest Abe. This monumental sculpture is surely something to gawk at for those new to the city. For home residents, it's just another interesting centerpiece that composes the place we call home.

Abe Lincoln's statue towers in at about 30 feet tall, wielding a trademark wooden axe. Created in 1968 by Springfield resident Carl Rinnus, the Rail Splitter statue is practically an immortalized landmark to contemporary Springfield society.

His pastel coloration and aged disposition serve as a reflection of Springfield as a timeless entity. Towering amongst the trees, it is quite the sight to behold. Feel free to take a barrage of photos with Abe while you're at it, he won't bite!

>TOURIST

34. MODERN ART STREWN THROUGHOUT – ACTS OF INTOLERANCE SCULPTURE

As beautiful as it is to picture spending the day gazing upon Abraham Lincoln's magnificent frame, Springfield holds more relevant pieces of art than the Rail Splitter Statue. Whether inside or out of a local art exhibit, each serves as a vital reflection of its composer's mindset and life experiences.

Quite the profound engraving, the Intolerance Sculpture located on 6th and Madison showcases a grave and tragic detail of profound weight. Each of the two statues of the Intolerance Sculpture represent a charred chimney rising from the smoldering ruins of once jovial buildings.

The images etched into these chimneys are based off blunt photos from the era that convey an echoic howl of infinite hardship. Composed by critically acclaimed artist Preston Jackson, the sculpture serves as a tribute to the horrors that occurred during the 1908 Race Riot in Springfield. As such, it serves as a vital piece of civil rights history.

Many other examples of civil rights pieces exist throughout the city, whether as landmarks or as features within art exhibits. Exploration is the key to sourcing the highest quality of said exhibits. The employees of most government-funded historic sites should serve as an incredibly helpful frame of reference as to where you can further your education in these topics.

35. STRUCTURAL BEAUTY OF BICENTENNIAL PLAZA

As with most major metropolitan areas and the like, Springfield has its own eye-candy Bicentennial Plaza. This walkway serves as a bridge between the Lincoln Home National Historic Site to the Illinois Governor's Mansion and Illinois State Capital. The statement that most places of importance in Springfield are clustered tightly knit together proves especially true with the plaza as an example.

The plaza once served as nothing more than a basic parking lot downtown. Nowadays, this property has found itself transformed into an archival showcase of Springfield's history in reference to the life of Abraham Lincoln.

>TOURIST

A lighting system on the plaza connects sixteen separate towers, each of which display different colors and patterns. These correlate with sixteen showcase panels that exist on the plaza, each detailing the events and lives of the people and places of Springfield. Bicentennial Plaza serves as an appetizer to the rich history of our active home.

Spots like these that are scattered throughout Springfield aid to uncover the more overshadowed elements of the region's history. Dig deep enough and you never know what you may discover.

36. SUPPORT OUR LOCAL SPORTS TEAMS

From the Jr. Blues, to the Sliders and the Senators, Springfield is chock full of high school/collegiate level sports events that unite the entire Midwest in competitive excitement. This extends likewise to renown teams such as the Lanphier Lions' basketball team, Sacred-Heart Griffin's football team, and many, many more. Smaller collegiate local teams exist in Springfield as well, so if you're up for some pickup games of rugby and some practice, go out of your way to make the connections! If you have the drive in you, you'll be sure to find yourself hanging with a good group of athletes in no time.

The Springfield Jr. Blues Hockey Club has persisted with excellent leadership for over 25 years. They are a Tier II Junior Hockey League, known for playing their home games at the Nelson Center's Jr. Blues Club/Rink, located at Lincoln Park. This franchise first joined the NAHL (North American Hockey League) for the '93-'94 season and have been going strong ever since.

The Springfield Sliders bleed green and radiate pride for their home city. Being a collegiate summer league baseball team, they are known for having won one championship since their 2007 formation as a franchise extension. Many former players of the Springfield Sliders later went on to compete in Major League Baseball. Most recently, the Sliders' Nick Maton of Chatham had been drafted to the Phillies in 2017.

Most high-school and collegiate teams in Springfield hold one or two alumni at the very least who served as essential factors to professional teams later in their lives. Widely famous alumni include

>TOURIST

Lanphier Lions' NBA All-Star 2012 and NBA Finals Most Valuable Player of 2015, Andre Iguodala.

37. OLD STATE CAPITOL

The capitol buildings of Springfield exist solely for the purpose of political management and employment. The Old State Capitol State Historic Site is the fifth capitol building for Illinois, home of many candidacy announcements from both the past and present. Abraham Lincoln, Barack Obama and Hillary Clinton are some of the many presidents and presidential candidates who have "held court" at the Old State Capitol.

In contemporary times, the Old State Capitol is also a refurnishing of what once was the fifth capitol building of Illinois. Architecture based from the Greek revival; the capital was reconstructed from the ground up during the 1960s. This location was also Lincoln's site where he lay-in-state during May 3-4, 1865.

The Old State Capital is accessible for people of all disabilities, as is the rest of the major government buildings in Illinois. The Old State

Capitol, as well as many other government sanctioned facilities are also good areas for the disabled to acquire long-term careers at, if they have the credentials/work experience to accommodate. Handicap accessibility compliance is truly a necessity for the modern day.

38. DANA-THOMAS HOUSE

Architecturally designed by Frank Lloyd Wright in 1902, the Dana-Thomas House was created for Springfield socialite Susan Lawrence Dana upon her receipt of a substantial heir. The house was built as a complete remodel of her family's old mansion. It was to serve as a projection of Dana's aspirations, doubling as a platform for her own agenda. The request for the Lawrence mansion to be rebuilt served as the most titanic request Wright was ever said to have taken on.

Nowadays, the Dana-Thomas House serves as yet another quintessential site of historical significance from within the city. The site is managed under the Illinois Historic Preservation Agency (IHPA) and is believed to contain the most intact of

Wright's interior designs. Restoration plans exist and are held by a third party.

By visiting the Dana-Thomas House, you'll be subjecting yourself to some of the more nuanced details of Springfield's history. Although it has been occasionally closed due to security issues and lack of funding, the house is open constantly nowadays and holds its rightful place as one of the go-to sites of interest in Springfield, Illinois. Like many other historic sites in the city, the Dana-Thomas house also hosts both meetings and seasonal events.

The accompanying Dana-Thomas House Foundation exists as a non-profit organization that seeks to build public interest in the lives and works of both Frank Lloyd Wright and Susan Lawrence Dana. This is done through public events that center around education and publication.

39. ABRAHAM LINCOLN MEMORIAL GARDEN

The Abraham Lincoln Memorial Garden is an autonomous botanical comprised of two sections: the 63-acre Jensen unit and the 29-acre Ostermeier

Prairie Center. Full-time staff at the garden include four men and women, as well as hundreds of volunteers. Each person you'll find frequenting the Abraham Lincoln Memorial Garden will be chock full of life and historic curiosity.

Housing six miles worth of astonishing trails can be found laced throughout the setting. In relation to the season, you're sure to experience a different environment every time depending.

In early Spring, the memorial garden is home to a some of the most Southern-oriented maple syrup festivals there ever were, or ever could be. Towards the end of Summer, a festival is held at the garden in honor of the leaves falling and taking their transition, along with the times.

Along with the plethora of activities and events, the garden also maintains not only its own year-round gift shop, but an equally active Nature Center as well.

From the majestic dogwoods to the beautiful views of Lake Springfield available at the garden, you'd be sure to regret not visiting this eye-catcher of a site. The Abraham Lincoln Memorial Garden is generally regarded as an undercover gem amongst Springfield's more overshadowing properties, sure to leave you awe-struck. Without a doubt, the garden is dedicated to family comfort and fun.

40. CENTRAL ILLINOIS AFRICAN AMERICAN HISTORY MUSEUM

Located in the heart of Springfield, the Central Illinois African American History Museum exists as a gallery to African American history and culture, specifically revolving that of Springfield. The location of this museum overtook what once was the Museum of Funeral Customs, which was closed sometime in late 2009. The museum is considered celebratory of African American history, rights, and cultural preservation.

The museum seeks to tell authentic stories in reference to African American life in Central Illinois. Similarly to the Dana-Thomas House Foundation, the museum can do this through scholarships, educational programs, partnerships, as well as via their financial supporters. The museum also supports interconnectivity and tolerance between all races.

Open Tuesday through Friday, the museum is an excellent place to further your education on the history of the civil rights movement, both past and present. As of recent, the museum holds an exhibit that displays the historically significant speeches of former president Barack Obama, with said speeches dating back as far as 2004. This correlates with their propensity for conveying historical importance orally, and as such proves as an important piece from within their catalog.

41. LINCOLN'S NEW SALEM

Lincoln's New Salem retains the location of New Salem City, where young Abraham Lincoln resided for six years, from 1831 to 1837. Labelled as New Salem in 1829, the settlement had existed for about twelve years before it was abandoned and left to deteriorate. The centerpiece of New Salem would be its creative recreation of the life-filled log village that once resided.

New Salem is open to the public within its operational hours, allowing for exploration at any pace. Signs on the log buildings convey detailing on

>TOURIST

the village's history, while interpreters dressed in period clothing can be seen throughout the village on most days, particularly during the tourist season.

As with the other historical sites in Springfield, New Salem is the host of many special events. Some of these events include New Salem's Candlewalk, live performances, quilting festivals and much, much more. A 500-seat outdoor theater of particular interest and prominence exists as well.

Overall, the New Salem Lincoln League (non-profit) serves its noble purpose of preserving a village that was once called Lincoln's home for many generations, both from the past and of the future.

42. VACHEL-LINDSAY HOME

The home of Vachel-Lindsay is yet another historic museum piece that resides in Springfield, awaiting the occupancy of our city's many tourists. Residing South of the Governor's Mansion, the Vachel-Lindsay Home provides a tangible echo of what once was the lives of Dr. Vachel Thomas Lindsay and his wife, Catharine Frazee. Originally a practicing doctor, Vachel Lindsay eventually became famous for his work as a poet. Lindsay was viewed as a somewhat controversial figure in the past, due to his co-signing for African American advocacy. Today, this serves as one of the many platforms that keep his name alive.

    Hosted by the IHPA, the Vachel-Lindsay home offers a torrent of events to the public in honor of the poet/doctor. Some of these events include the "Poets in the Parlor" series, as well as the "Artist in Residence" exhibits. Many lectures and workshops meant for educators, historians as well as the general public are provided via this location as well. This spot is most suitable for those interested in writing plus the life details of the doctor and his influence upon modern society.

    Some works of the doctor's I would keep an eye out for would include Going to the Sun, as well as Abraham Lincoln Walks at Midnight. Vachel-Lindsay is the modern originator of what is referred to as "singing poetry", which is poetry created with the sole intention of being chanted or sung. The origin of this genre is further elaborated upon through various exhibits in the museum.

>TOURIST

43. BOTANICAL GARDENS

Centerfold around recreation as well as education, the Springfield Park District's Washington Park Botanical Garden is the perfect locale for a family field trip. With the majority of Springfield being deeply entrenched in modernization, the Botanical Garden is a much-needed breath of fresh air that compliments its neighboring landmarks.

Both annual and perennial flower beds lace the entirety of the visual, leaving the perfect scene for introspection. From the magnificent fragrance of the Rose Garden to the eye-catching "pop" of the evergreen trees and their Earthen shade.

Washington Park Botanical Garden aims to preserve not only its garden, but the balance of nature in general through education. Multiple times a year there are educational events and school tours (pre-k through college level) free of charge. A large amount of documentation regarding horticultural information exists as well, along with accompanying plant galleries.

The elegant sanctuary known as Springfield's Botanical Garden includes 20 acres of land with over 1800 species of plants, each sorted into ten specific garden areas and a Conservatory. Attached to the garden is an additional 9000 sq. ft, with the purpose of housing an indoor greenhouse area.

Endearing seasonal displays include Japanese bonsai trees, orchids and Easter lilies. There's nothing more welcoming than a little bit of festivity. To crank up the festivities a notch, Washington Park Botanical Garden offers its setting as an outdoor wedding area in Springfield. Likewise, the venue can be rented for multiple purposes.

Rentals at the Botanical Garden occupy the exhibit hall.

In terms of philanthropy, the Springfield Angel of Hope, NFP (non-profit) bestowed an Angel of Hope Statue in the Washington Park Botanical Garden. This statue serves as a monument to all who grieve for a lost child in their life. 300+ names are added to the statue annually. Nationwide, more than 100 communities have installed or are in the process of having an Angel of Hope statue installed. Seven of these Angel of Hope statues were erected in Illinois.

>TOURIST

44. ELIJAH ILES HOUSE

Getting tired of all the historic houses yet? Well, fear not! We have plenty, plenty more to address here before the book is over. The Elijah Iles House is a historic house located in Springfield, Illinois. This majestic house was first built in 1837 and has remained there ever since. As such, the Elijah Iles house is indeed the oldest residential structure to exist today. The home's occupant, Elijah Isles, was one of our city's earliest settlers. His stay in Springfield began in 1821.

Elijah was known for running the first store in Sangamon County, an accomplishment that paved the way for the future of our city's industrialization. He also served as a major during the Winnebago War of 1827. While enlisted as a private during the Black Hawk War (later to be promoted to captain), Elijah led Abraham Lincoln from within his unit at one point.

The house itself is based off Greek Revival design, further inspired by Southern architecture. Almost to be regarded as a time capsule, the house is one of the few examples of Greek Revival remaining in Springfield. Three levels of awe-inspiring construct, the Elijah Iles house tells a visual and oral history that will resonate for lifetimes to come.

45. EDWARDS PLACE HISTORIC HOME

Pairing perfectly with the mention of the Elijah Iles House, Edwards Place is yet another historic house located in our prominent city. This structure would serve as a twin example of the Greek Revival style, channeling resolve to the dying spirit of said logistics. Construction began sometime in 1833, making it just one year younger than its main contemporary. Additions were made in 1836 and 1843, accompanied by a meticulous expansion in 1857. Edwards Place remains today as it was since its final add-on.

Famous lawyer Benjamin S. Edwards, son of an Illinois governor, owned the house in which we reference. During his stay at the home, he found the domain becoming a catalyst for quite a plethora of political activities in Springfield. Here, he was able to host rallies and gatherings for Illinois politicians. Most famously, Edwards Place is known for having

>TOURIST

been the grounds in which Abraham Lincoln gave one of his critically acclaimed speeches from the second story.

The house was donated to the Springfield Art Association 1913 and has served as a community center ever since. In 1969, Edwards Place was added to the National Register of Historic Places.

46. ILLINOIS STATE MUSEUM

The state museum here in Springfield is a bombastic showcase of all angles and aspects of Illinois culture. Once free, the Illinois State Museum was unfortunately closed for the time periods of October 2015 through June 2016. By July 2016, the museum was able to reopen via adopting an admission fee. This fee is fully waived for both children and veterans, leaving the museum accessible to those who may find interest in it the most. However, the fee is well worth paying likewise in order to get a glimpse at days passed in Illinois. Important satellite locations to visit during your stay include Dickson Mounds, Lockport Gallery, and the ISM Chicago Gallery.

The Dickson Mounds Museum in Lewistown is a worthy tribute to the culture of Native Americans in Illinois, as well as their long-term influence on today's society. Interactive displays, dioramas and artifacts lay beckoning your discovery, each with a unique story to tell. The eras depicted range from the Ice Age to the 19th Century. The Illinois State Museum contains its own Native American exhibits as well.

Lockport and ISM Chicago Galleries revolve around both past and contemporary artists and artisans who lived in Illinois. Interesting facts include that the Lockport Gallery functioned as a grain-processing facility until the 1950s.

47. GOVERNOR'S MANSION

Current Governor of Illinois, J.B. Pritzker, resides in the Governor's Mansion located on E. Jackson Street. Having been built in 1855, the Governor's Mansion of Illinois happens to be one of the oldest standing mansions of this distinction in the entire United States. The mansion was designed by Chicago architect John M. Van Osdel.

>TOURIST

Lavish decorations are laid about the mansion grounds during holidays, with the house non-seasonally functioning as a house museum. Many meetings and events occur here, with the sitting Governor and his family's stay at the mansion not being enforced by the law, thus giving them housing freedom. The majority of the building's architecture is maintained as to represent the 19th century and its stylistics. Most of the mansion's furniture was refurbished during Governor George Ryan's 1999-2003 run. Private funds were used in 2019 yet again for restoration of the mansion, including renovations to guest rooms, fixtures and plumbing.

48. LINCOLN'S TOMB

A tale of historic resonance is to be told in reference to Lincoln's Tomb, a site infamous for its past reputation as a graverobber's haven. The tomb is the final resting place of Abraham Lincoln and his wife Mary, as well as three out of four of their sons. The tomb can be found in Oak Ridge cemetery, deep within the enticing atmosphere of Lincoln Park.

Built between 1868 and 1874, this peculiar tomb was constructed entirely of granite, containing many surrounding adornments and decorations. The single-story base of the tomb is overshadowed by an enormous obelisk. A multitude of busts and statues of Lincoln and related scenes were carefully erected amongst the monumental grave site.

Extensive reconstruction took place between the years of 1900 and 1901, only to be recanted one last time amidst 1930 and 1931. Some changes made include an entire redesign of the interior tomb.

The coffin of Abraham Lincoln was relocated from its initial placement to where it is today (below burial chamber floor) after the first renovation. This is due to the bodysnatching attempt of 1876. Make sure to visit the Lincoln Library if you're interested in learning more, as my brief synopsis couldn't begin to explain the rabbit-hole that is this topic.

49. MR. ACCORDION'S GRAVE

Oak Ridge Cemetery, the scenic home to Lincoln's Tomb, happens to hold its own exclusive, non-Lincoln related tales as well. The Mr. Accordion

> TOURIST

in question was a man by the name of Roy Bertelli, an enigma of a man who dreamed of being buried in Oak Ridge cemetery. One day, a plot was made available, and Roy happily purchased said plot. The story goes on through a series of twist and turns litigation-wise, which slow Roy's quest to attain this grave plot down like quicksand.

Eventually though, Roy manages to slight-of-hand (well-deservedly) his way into retaining his beloved burial site. Upon achieving this, due to all the stress and heartache of gaining this spot, "Mr. Accordion" decided to channel this negative energy into leaving his mark on Springfield. He built a crypt above ground in Oak Ridge, erecting a ginormous tablet with an engraved accordion over it, all accompanied by bouncing musical notes.

Not much else to really say about the local legend that is the tale of Mr. Accordion and his Tomb of Defiance. For those who are fans of lore-oriented places (think New Jersey) and historical mythos, you are sure to spin quite the tale in your own head while visiting the infamous tomb. I can guarantee that hundreds, if not thousands of little stories like this exist all throughout the resting grounds of many a Springfieldian.

50. COME BACK AGAIN SOON!

Wow, you know, to me it seemed as though you just arrived here yesterday! What'd you think of the place? Did you like the food? Would you come back again? Well, I'm glad to hear that! Springfield is an absolute nexus to most the important entertainment events and attractions that occur within the Midwest. To not visit Springfield as someone who frequents said region would be doing yourself a massive disservice.

Historical landmarks and friendly faces galore, Springfield may just provide the well-needed vacation that you deserve! One of the best things about Springfield is that, depending on where you are at, it has a little piece of home for everyone, no matter your place of origin! Our humble city does an excellent job at providing cultural backdrop for anyone and everyone with good intentions.

>TOURIST

TOP REASONS TO BOOK THIS TRIP

Nightlife: Springfield is an amazing intermediary to spend a weekend or two at with your friends! You're sure to get into lots of trouble, but always make it out alive with experiences and stories that will last a lifetime.

Food: Illinois' capital is renowned for its smorgasbord of lower-end and higher-scale restaurants throughout the entirety of the city. You won't manage to hit every fantastic spot in one trip, so be prepared to schedule several more!

Cultural Prominence: From modern art to historical landmarks, the city serves as the quintessential learning experience for travelers everywhere. This proves double true for historians, as the capital is after all, the home of former president Abraham Lincoln.

>TOURIST

"I like to see a man proud of the place in which he lives. I like to see a man live so that his place will be proud of him."

– Abraham Lincoln

OTHER RESOURCES:

- Sites and Hotel Maps: https://visitspringfieldillinois.com/Images/Getting Around/2016SpringfieldVisitorMap.pdf
- Bike/Hike Trails: https://visitspringfieldillinois.com/ThingsToDo/Recreation.aspx?Bike
- Springfield Mass Transit Buses: http://www.smtd.org/
- Taxis in Springfield: https://www.yellowpages.com/springfield-il/taxis
- Interstate Route Map: https://visitspringfieldillinois.com/Images/Getting Around/directional.gif
- Springfield, Illinois Google Maps: https://www.google.com/maps/place/Springfield,+IL

>TOURIST

PACKING AND PLANNING TIPS

A Week before Leaving

- Arrange for someone to take care of pets and water plants.
- Email and Print important Documents.
- Get Visa and vaccines if needed.
- Check for travel warnings.
- Stop mail and newspaper.
- Notify Credit Card companies where you are going.
- Passports and photo identification is up to date.
- Pay bills.
- Copy important items and download travel Apps.
- Start collecting small bills for tips.
- Have post office hold mail while you are away.
- Check weather for the week.
- Car inspected, oil is changed, and tires have the correct pressure.
- Check airline luggage restrictions.
- Download Apps needed for your trip.

Right Before Leaving

- Contact bank and credit cards to tell them your location.
- Clean out refrigerator.
- Empty garbage cans.
- Lock windows.
- Make sure you have the proper identification with you.
- Bring cash for tips.
- Remember travel documents.
- Lock door behind you.
- Remember wallet.
- Unplug items in house and pack chargers.
- Change your thermostat settings.
- Charge electronics, and prepare camera memory cards.

\>TOURIST

READ OTHER GREATER THAN A TOURIST BOOKS

Greater Than a Tourist- Geneva Switzerland: 50 Travel Tips from a Local by Amalia Kartika

Greater Than a Tourist- St. Croix US Birgin Islands USA: 50 Travel Tips from a Local by Tracy Birdsall

Greater Than a Tourist- San Juan Puerto Rico: 50 Travel Tips from a Local by Melissa Tait

Greater Than a Tourist – Lake George Area New York USA: 50 Travel Tips from a Local by Janine Hirschklau

Greater Than a Tourist – Monterey California United States: 50 Travel Tips from a Local by Katie Begley

Greater Than a Tourist – Chanai Crete Greece: 50 Travel Tips from a Local by Dimitra Papagrigoraki

Greater Than a Tourist – The Garden Route Western Cape Province South Africa: 50 Travel Tips from a Local by Li-Anne McGregor van Aardt

Greater Than a Tourist – Sevilla Andalusia Spain: 50 Travel Tips from a Local by Gabi Gazon

Children's Book: *Charlie the Cavalier Travels the World* by Lisa Rusczyk Ed. D.

> TOURIST

Follow us on Instagram for beautiful travel images:
http://Instagram.com/GreaterThanATourist

Follow *Greater Than a Tourist* on Amazon.

>Tourist Podcast
>T Website
>T Youtube
>T Facebook
>T Goodreads
>T Amazon
>T Mailing List
>T Pinterest
>T Instagram
>T Twitter
>T SoundCloud
>T LinkedIn
>T Map

> TOURIST

At *Greater Than a Tourist*, we love to share travel tips with you. How did we do? What guidance do you have for how we can give you better advice for your next trip? Please send your feedback to GreaterThanaTourist@gmail.com as we continue to improve the series. We appreciate your constructive feedback. Thank you.

>TOURIST

METRIC CONVERSIONS

TEMPERATURE

- 110° F — 40° C
- 100° F
- 90° F — 30° C
- 80° F
- 70° F — 20° C
- 60° F
- 50° F — 10° C
- 40° F
- 32° F — 0° C
- 20° F
- 10° F — -10° C
- 0° F — -18° C
- -10° F
- -20° F — -30° C

To convert F to C:

Subtract 32, and then multiply by 5/9 or .5555.

To Convert C to F:

Multiply by 1.8 and then add 32.

32F = 0C

LIQUID VOLUME

To Convert:	Multiply by
U.S. Gallons to Liters	3.8
U.S. Liters to Gallons	.26
Imperial Gallons to U.S. Gallons	1.2
Imperial Gallons to Liters	4.55
Liters to Imperial Gallons	.22

1 Liter = .26 U.S. Gallon
1 U.S. Gallon = 3.8 Liters

DISTANCE

To convert	Multiply by
Inches to Centimeters	2.54
Centimeters to Inches	.39
Feet to Meters	.3
Meters to Feet	3.28
Yards to Meters	.91
Meters to Yards	1.09
Miles to Kilometers	1.61
Kilometers to Miles	.62

1 Mile = 1.6 km
1 km = .62 Miles

WEIGHT

1 Ounce = .28 Grams
1 Pound = .4555 Kilograms
1 Gram = .04 Ounce
1 Kilogram = 2.2 Pounds

\>TOURIST

TRAVEL QUESTIONS

- Do you bring presents home to family or friends after a vacation?
- Do you get motion sick?
- Do you have a favorite billboard?
- Do you know what to do if there is a flat tire?
- Do you like a sun roof open?
- Do you like to eat in the car?
- Do you like to wear sun glasses in the car?
- Do you like toppings on your ice cream?
- Do you use public bathrooms?
- Did you bring a cell phone and does it have power?
- Do you have a form of identification with you?
- Have you ever been pulled over by a cop?
- Have you ever given money to a stranger on a road trip?
- Have you ever taken a road trip with animals?
- Have you ever gone on a vacation alone?
- Have you ever run out of gas?

- If you could move to any place in the world, where would it be?

- If you could travel anywhere in the world, where would you travel?

- If you could travel in any vehicle, which one would it be?

- If you had three things to wish for from a magic genie, what would they be?

- If you have a driver's license, how many times did it take you to pass the test?

- What are you the most afraid of on vacation?

- What do you want to get away from the most when you are on vacation?

- What foods smell bad to you?

- What item do you bring on ever trip with you away from home?

- What makes you sleepy?

- What song would you love to hear on the radio when you're cruising on the highway?

- What travel job would you want the least?

- What will you miss most while you are away from home?

- What is something you always wanted to try?

>TOURIST

- What is the best road side attraction that you ever saw?
- What is the farthest distance you ever biked?
- What is the farthest distance you ever walked?
- What is the weirdest thing you needed to buy while on vacation?
- What is your favorite candy?
- What is your favorite color car?
- What is your favorite family vacation?
- What is your favorite food?
- What is your favorite gas station drink or food?
- What is your favorite license plate design?
- What is your favorite restaurant?
- What is your favorite smell?
- What is your favorite song?
- What is your favorite sound that nature makes?
- What is your favorite thing to bring home from a vacation?
- What is your favorite vacation with friends?
- What is your favorite way to relax?

- Where is the farthest place you ever traveled in a car?

- Where is the farthest place you ever went North, South, East and West?

- Where is your favorite place in the world?

- Who is your favorite singer?

- Who taught you how to drive?

- Who will you miss the most while you are away?

- Who if the first person you will contact when you get to your destination?

- Who brought you on your first vacation?

- Who likes to travel the most in your life?

- Would you rather be hot or cold?

- Would you rather drive above, below, or at the speed limited?

- Would you rather drive on a highway or a back road?

- Would you rather go on a train or a boat?

- Would you rather go to the beach or the woods?

>TOURIST

TRAVEL BUCKET LIST

1.

2.

3.

4.

5.

6.

7.

8.

9.

10.

>TOURIST

NOTES

Made in the USA
Monee, IL
25 November 2024